THE COLLAPSE OF COTTON TENANCY

THE COLLAPSE OF COTTON TENANCY

Summary of
Field Studies & Statistical Surveys 1933-35

BY

CHARLES S. JOHNSON · EDWIN R. EMBREE
W. W. ALEXANDER

Chapel Hill
THE UNIVERSITY OF NORTH CAROLINA PRESS
1935

NOTE

A COMMISSION OF THREE has made during the past two years an intensive study of cotton culture and farm tenancy in the region commonly known as the Old South. The detailed investigations have been carried out by corps of students, under the direction of Dr. Rupert B. Vance and his colleagues of the University of North Carolina Institute for Research in Social Science, and of Professor Charles S. Johnson and his associates in the Department of Social Science of Fisk University. Full reports of these studies are in course of editing and publication. The present brief summary of the findings of this extensive research is issued for general readers who may not care to delve into the intricacies of a complex subject, but who, as citizens, should know the outlines of a significant and tragic situation which is of immediate concern to public policy.

This summary, while based chiefly on the findings of our own recent field studies, is authenticated by many previous reports. Footnote references to authorities are omitted in order to conserve the time and attention of the general reader. The more important of the publications which we have used are listed in the selected bibliography at the back of the volume.

PREFACE

FARM tenancy is an age-old curse of agriculture in many parts of the world. Yet the experience of Denmark and Ireland and other European countries is encouraging evidence that tenancy, even when it is an established custom, can be supplanted successfully by individual ownership.

The American ideal is that each citizen shall have the opportunity to work out his own career and to progress mentally, morally, and financially as far as his talents and his industry will carry him. To an extent probably beyond that of any other nation, we in this new country have been able to realize this ideal. But occasionally systems grow up, even in this land of opportunity, which make it almost impossible for individuals—for great groups of individuals—to make any headway or even to prevent themselves from sinking lower and lower. One of the worst of our economic quagmires is the system of farm tenancy or share cropping.

This booklet is the report of an intensive study of this tenancy system in one of its most acute phases, that of cotton culture. While we assume no responsibility for the detailed statements in the report, we believe that every conscientious study of the situation should be earnestly considered by the American people so that they may arouse themselves to destroy the evils of this system. Regardless of political leanings, all intelligent and humane citizens unite in wishing to see tenancy transformed into independence. A better distribution of farm ownership will mean a better balanced agriculture with more attention to nourishing food crops for the farmers' own use and less to purely commercial products. Greatly enlarged opportunity for hundreds of thousands of present dependent tenants to own their farms is a move toward social justice and toward individual independence in the best American tradition.

George Foster Peabody, New York, and Warm Springs, Georgia

Samuel McCrea Cavert, Federal Council of Churches, New York

William Green, American Federation of Labor, Washington, D. C.

Clark Howell, *The Atlanta Constitution*, Atlanta, Georgia

Benjamin Hubert, Georgia State Industrial College, Savannah, Georgia

Governor Frank O. Lowden, Oregon, Illinois

R. R. Moton, Tuskegee, Alabama

F. E. Murphy, *The Tribune*, Minneapolis, Minnesota

Howard Odum, University of North Carolina, Chapel Hill, North Carolina

Charlton Ogburn, American Federation of Labor, Washington, D. C.

Clarence Poe, *The Progressive Farmer*, Raleigh, North Carolina

B. Kirk Rankin, *Southern Agriculturist*, Nashville, Tennessee

Rt. Rev. Msgr. John A. Ryan, National Catholic Welfare Conference, Washington, D. C.

Rev. Edgar Schmiedeler, National Catholic Welfare Conference, Washington, D. C.

Edgar B. Stern, New Orleans, Louisiana

William Allen White, Emporia, Kansas

General Robert E. Wood, President, Sears, Roebuck and Company, Chicago, Illinois

TABLE OF CONTENTS

THE COLLAPSE OF COTTON TENANCY

I

COTTON TENANCY

COTTON has been the most important American commercial crop. It is linked historically with many of our characteristic institutions: the plantation system, the rise and collapse of slavery, and, to an amazing degree, with the culture of the entire South. For more than a century, this greatest of economic assets has been also our greatest social humiliation. The Kingdom of Cotton, reared first upon the backs of black slaves, is supported today by an ever-increasing horde of white and black tenants and share-croppers whose lives are hopelessly broken by the system. Although adding a billion dollars annually to the wealth of the world, the cotton farmers themselves are the most impoverished and backward of any large group of producers in America.

The cotton tenants live at the level of mere subsistence. But they are not the only sufferers under the evil despotism of King Cotton. The devotion to a single crop has left the whole region of the Old South dependent upon the fluctuations of one commodity, at the mercy of the success of a single plant. Continuous tilling of one crop has worn out soil over wide areas which previously were rich and fertile. Devotion to a commercial harvest has left an abundant farm region destitute of food crops, and its people living on a shockingly meager and ill-balanced diet.

The past five years of economic depression have accentuated the problems and aggravated the evils of American cotton culture. Changes in world markets and the development of substitute materials now threaten the life of the industry. The growth of cotton in the Southwest, and the prospect of increasing use of machinery in tilling and picking, make it certain that the ancient order of cotton culture in the Old South is doomed. Sweeping changes in southern farming must come swiftly if millions of former plantation workers are not to be completely wrecked—if the region itself is not to suffer violent ruin.

THE COTTON BELT

The cotton belt as determined by soil, climate, and rainfall, lies between 25° and 37° north latitude. Cotton culture now occupies a belt 300 miles north and south, stretching 1,600 miles from the Carolinas to western Texas. In this area 125 million acres are devoted to this single crop—nearly as great an amount of land as is given to all other crops together in this huge region.

Until the Civil War cotton was produced chiefly under the plantation system with slave labor. Free or white workers had no place on the old plantations. The presence or absence of cotton culture largely determined the racial distribution of the population in American settlement during the period from the middle of the 18th to the middle of the 19th century. Negro slavery and cotton grew up together in the Old South, beginning in the Carolinas, which were most typical of cotton culture and the plantation order a century or more ago. But this one crop system, essentially exploitative of the soil, always found it easier to move westward to newer land than to preserve or restore the old farms. Thus the cotton area, carrying slavery and the plantation with it, moved steadily to Georgia and Alabama, then on to Tennessee, Mississippi, and Louisiana. More recently, with the former slaves simply transformed into almost equally dependent tenants, and with ever increasing numbers of white laborers drawn into the meshes of tenancy, the cotton area has moved on westward to Texas, Arkansas, Oklahoma, and finally to southern California. Expansion westward proceeded very gradually until after 1910, when, at the time of the World War, came a tremendous expansion of the Southwest.

The belt is marked by dense farm populations. While the South, as a whole, is the most thickly populated rural area in America, the cotton belt is the most densely peopled region in the South. Negroes, remaining from slavery times, contribute large numbers to the older sections, forming over forty per cent of the total inhabitants of South Carolina, Georgia, and Alabama, and slightly more than half the population of Mississippi. But Negroes no longer make up the bulk of cotton tenants. White workers, in an increasing flood, have been drawn into the cotton fields, until today they outnumber the blacks more than five to three.

TENANCY

In the ten chief cotton states over sixty per cent of those engaged in the production of this crop are tenants. The computations of Rupert B. Vance place the number of tenant families in the cotton belt at 1,790,783. Of these, 1,091,944 are white, and 698,839 are colored. The family units of white tenants are larger than the colored, due in part to the earlier break-up of Negro families and the high infant death rate. The total number of individuals in these tenant families runs to approximately five and a half million whites and slightly over three million Negroes.

Tenancy for decades has been steadily increasing. The number of farms operated by tenants in the South was high enough in 1880, when 36.2 per cent were run by tenants. By 1920 the percentage of tenancy had

reached 49.6, and in 1930 it was 55.5. These figures are
for the South as a whole. In the cotton belt the percentage of tenancy is still higher. Out of every hundred cotton farms, over sixty are operated by tenants.

Up to the Civil War cotton laborers universally were
Negro slaves. It is one of the strange facts of the history of the slave period that white non-slaveholding
families, in spite of their numbers and their destitution,
were given no place in the expanding cotton culture,
save where they were able to hang on to the fringes
of the industry as overseers or as small independent
farmers. After Emancipation, however, white families
began to compete with Negroes for the new kind of
slavery involved in tenancy. The white tenants have
increased steadily, filling the new openings in the expanding industry, and taking places left vacant by Negroes who migrated from the plantations to northern
and southern cities. In the decade from 1920 to 1930,
white tenants in the cotton states increased by 200,000
families—approximately a million persons. During the
same decade Negro tenants decreased by 2,000 families
as a result of mass movements to cities. Since 1914, this
Negro migration to the North alone has exceeded a
million and a half persons. Increasingly, therefore, the
problems of the rural South in general, and of cotton
tenancy in particular, are those of native white families
much more than of Negroes.

What Is a Tenant?

A farm tenant, in the widest meaning of the term, is any person who hires the farm which he operates, paying for the use of the land either by a share of the crop which he raises or by cash rental or both. Now the renting of land is not in itself a bad thing; it is customary in other parts of America and to a limited extent in Europe. It is a simple means of getting access to land by persons who have not capital enough to purchase farms. Normally it is regarded as a step on the road to independent ownership. The evil is not in renting land but in the traditions and practices which have grown up about it in the South.

Tenants may be divided into three main classes: (a) renters who hire land for a fixed rental to be paid either in cash or its equivalent in crop values; (b) share tenants, who furnish their own farm equipment and work animals and obtain use of land by agreeing to pay a fixed per cent of the cash crop which they raise; (c) share-croppers who have to have furnished to them not only the land but also farm tools and animals, fertilizer, and often even the food they consume, and who in return pay a larger per cent of the crop.

In considering cotton tenancy, the first group may be almost ignored. Those who have definite agreements with landlords as to exact rental prices are few in number and their status is so independent as to remove them from the system of subservient tenancy. The share tenants and share-croppers are the two great subdivisions of the dependent workers in the cotton belt. The difference between these two classes is simply one of degree. The share tenants, since they supply much of their own equipment, are able to rent the land on fairly good terms, usually on the basis of paying to the owner not more than one-fourth or one-third of the crop raised. The share-croppers, on the other hand, having almost nothing to offer but their labor, must pay as rent a higher share of the product, usually one-half of the crop. In addition, of course, both tenants and croppers must pay out of their share of the crop for all that is supplied to them in the way of seed, fertilizer, and food supplies. "Tenancy," as used in the present report and as commonly applied in the South, is a general term covering both the share tenants and the share-croppers, but not the renters. As a matter of fact, over one-third of all tenants in the South, and over half of the Negro tenants are croppers, that is, in the lowest category of poverty and dependence.

The risk of the tenant increases, of course, in proportion to what he is able to contribute to the contract. There is almost no financial risk assumed by the share cropper who furnishes only his labor (and that of his family), who receives his equipment and supplies and even his food, from the owner. The share tenant, who supplies his own tools and work animals, assumes more risk, and in return expects a larger share of the earnings. The renter of course assumes much greater risk. In turn the landlord's potential profits increase as he assumes more and more of the risk. Therein lies a danger to the tenant. It is to the advantage of the owner to encourage the most dependent form of share cropping as a source of largest profits. And he wishes to hold in greatest dependence just those workers who are most efficient. A shiftless and inefficient cropper is of little value to the owner and is expelled, unless, in a serious labor shortage, absence of any worker is even more costly than the presence of an incompetent one. The industrious and thrifty tenant is sought by the landlord. The very qualities which might normally lead a tenant to attain the position of renter, and eventually of owner, are just the ones which make him a permanent asset as a cropper. Landlords, thus, are most concerned with maintaining the system that furnishes them labor and that keeps this labor under their control, that is, in the tenancy class. The means by which landowners do this are: first, the credit system; and second, the established social customs of the plantation order.

As a part of the age-old custom in the South, the landlord keeps the books and handles the sale of all the crops. The owner returns to the cropper only what is left over of his share of the profits after deductions for all items which the landlord has advanced to him during the year: seed, fertilizer, working equipment, and food supplies, plus interest on all this indebtedness, plus a theoretical "cost of supervision." The landlord often supplies the food—"pantry supplies" or "furnish"—and other current necessities through his own store or commissary. Fancy prices at the commissary, exorbitant interest, and careless or manipulated accounts, make it easy for the owner to keep his tenants constantly in debt.

The plight of the tenant at annual settlement time is so common that a whole folklore about it has grown up in the South.

A tenant offering five bales of cotton was told, after some owl-eyed figuring, that this cotton exactly balanced his debt. Delighted at the prospect of a profit this year, the tenant reported that he had one more bale which he hadn't yet brought in. "Shucks," shouted the boss, "why didn't you tell me before? Now I'll have to figure the account all over again to make it come out even."

Of course every story of this kind, and such stories are innumerable, can be matched by tales of unreliability and shiftlessness on the part of the tenant. The case against the system cannot be rested on any personal indictment of landlords any more than it can be vindicated by stories of the improvidence of tenants. The fact is that landlords generally act as they find it necessary to act under the system; tenants do likewise. The development of bad economic and social habits of whatever kind on the part of both landlords and tenants is direct evidence of a faulty system.

Even more than the credit system, the traditions of the region hold the tenant in thrall. The plantation system developed during slavery. It continues on the old master and slave pattern. For many years, even after Emancipation, black tenants were the rule in the cotton fields and the determination to "keep the Negro in his place" was, if anything, stronger after the Civil War than before. Although white families now form the great majority of the cotton tenants, the old "boss and black" attitude still pervades the whole system. Because of his economic condition, and because of his race, color, and previous condition of servitude, the rural Negro is helpless before the white master. Every kind of exploitation and abuse is permitted because of the old caste prejudice. The poor white connives in this abuse of the Negro; in fact, he is the most violent protagonist of it. This fixed custom of exploitation of the Negro has carried over to the white tenant and cropper. Yet it has been impossible to bring about any change, even to get the poor white workers to take a stand, since any movement for reform is immediately confused with the race issue. Because of their insistence upon the degrading of three million Negro tenants, five

and a half million white workers continue to keep themselves in virtual peonage.

WHAT THE TENANT EARNS

The average American farm family in 1929 earned
$1,240, and this was about a third of the average for
non-farm families. The lowest general earnings were in
the southern states. The Carolinas, Mississippi, Arkansas, Alabama, Georgia, and Tennessee, the states of the
old cotton belt, stood at the bottom of the list. Here,
even at the period of national prosperity, a vast farm
population barely earned subsistence.

Every study of wages and income in the South makes
perfectly clear the low economic position of the rural
South. Clarence Heer's exhaustive study of wages and
income, covering a period of thirty years, showed that
southern agriculture had provided its farmers just about
half the per capita income of farmers in other sections.
This includes all the "independent farmers, plantation
owners, tenants, and share croppers." When tenants
alone are considered, the family earnings slump distress-
ingly below the level of decent subsistence.

The debts are a part of the system and are of two
kinds: those accumulating from year to year; and current debts arising from the "furnishing" system. More
than a third of the tenants have debts of more than a
year's standing. In six widely differing counties included in the field studies of our Committee, 43.4 per

cent of the tenants were in debt before they planted their 1934 crop. The average indebtedness, according to the Alabama tenants who were able to keep any record of their accounts, was $80.00.

As to current earnings or deficits, a study of Negro tenant farmers in Macon County, Alabama, in 1932, published in *Shadow of the Plantation*, showed that 61.7 per cent "broke even," 26.0 per cent "went in the hole," and 9.4 per cent made some profit. Of this latter group the total income ranged from about $70 to $90 per year. The special inquiry into tenant farmer earnings by this Committee, which covered some 2,000 families in 1934 and 1935 in Mississippi, Texas, Alabama, and South Carolina, found variations in earnings according to soil fertility and types of management, but universally a sub-standard. Inseparable from the small gross earnings of these farmers was the stern factor of landlord policy, prerogative, alleged supervision charges, and interest rates. It must be remembered that the tenant's actual income is very different from the earnings of his farm as listed in agricultural reports. The landlord's share is taken from the earnings together with the operator's gross expenses.

For the small number of all these 2,000 tenant families who received a cash income in 1933, the average was $105.43. The actual earnings per family, when distributed among five persons, would give a monthly income per person of $1.75. And these incomes, theoretically at least, were benefiting from the federal program of aid to farmers as administered in 1933.

Tenants in general have to consider themselves fortunate if they can farm for subsistence only. One cropper complained dismally: "For 18 years we ain't cleared a thing or made any real money." Another had received his cash in a manner which made it difficult to remember the amounts: "I couldn't possibly go to task and tell you. I got it in dribbles and couldn't keep a record of it, but it wasn't over $75.00." Still another farmer "cleared $45.00 last year; nothing the year before and no settlement; cleared $117.00 the year before that. The most I ever cleared was $260.00—just before the war." Few of the tenants interviewed had cleared cash incomes since 1921, and many had made nothing since the World War.

There could, perhaps, be some compensation for low incomes if the farms were supplying food for the families. But the production of a cash crop rules out the raising of general produce. This much is obvious: if there is any advantage in cotton farming as a profitable business, the tenant does not share it.

How the Tenant Lives

Cotton has always been a cheap-labor crop; its development has rested on keeping this labor cost low. In fact many declare that profit is impossible "if all the labor it requires were paid for." The results appear in the living standards of the millions of families whose men, women, and children produce the crop.

The cultural landscape of the cotton belt has been described as a "miserable panorama of unpainted shacks, rain-gullied fields, straggling fences, rattle-trap Fords, dirt, poverty, disease, drudgery, and monotony that stretches for a thousand miles across the cotton belt." It used to be said that "cotton is and must remain a black man's crop, not a white man's, because the former's standard of living has always been low, and his natural inferiority makes it unnecessary to change it." Now that white families make up nearly two-thirds of the workers, it is clear that meager and pinched living is not a racial trait but a result of the system of cotton tenancy. Submerged beneath the system which he supports, the cotton tenant's standard of living approaches the level of bare animal existence. The traditional status of the slave required only subsistence. The cotton slave—white or colored—has inherited a rôle in which comfort, education, and self-development have no place. For the type of labor he performs, all that is actually required is a stomach indifferently filled, a shack to sleep in, some old jeans to cover his nakedness.

This age-old condition of the cotton worker and the necessity to keep it unchanged, lead to some interesting rationalizing by supporters of the existing order. Serious statements about the happiness of the tenant in his dependent rôle are taking the place of the earlier stories of the contentment of the slaves. Anecdotes of ludicrous spending whenever he gets his hands on money are used to justify the regular condition of poverty. Shiftlessness and laziness are reported as reasons for the dependent state, whereas, in fact, in so far as they exist, they are not necessarily inherent, but are caused by the very conditions of the share-cropping system.

The studies made of tenant families confirm the indignant assertion of a writer in the Dallas, Texas, *News* that "the squalid condition of the cotton raisers of the South is a disgrace to the southern people. They stay in shacks, thousands of which are unfit to house animals, much less human beings. Their children are born under such conditions of medical treatment, food and clothing, as would make an Eskimo rejoice that he did not live in a cotton growing country."

The drab ugliness of tenant houses might be condoned if they were comfortable. Many of them are old, some have actually come down from the period of slavery, and all of them, unpainted and weather-beaten, appear ageless. They are crudely constructed, windows and doors are out of alignment, they leak even while still new. Family size and size of house have no relationship. Whatever the number in the family it must occupy the customary three rooms. In fact a family of any size may live in a two-room house; as many as thirteen have been found living in a single bedroom and kitchen.

A Children's Bureau study of the welfare of children in cotton-growing areas of Texas, showed 64 per cent of the white and 77 per cent of the Negro families living under conditions of housing congestion, and this in spite of the common belief that over-crowding is a phenomenon of the city. Another study of white tenant families in Tennessee estimated an average value of all personal belongings of tenants at less than a hundred dollars. In one cotton-growing county of Alabama, reported in *Shadow of the Plantation*, over half of the families lived in one- and two-room cabins, and the comment on the character and inadequacy of these by one of the tenants does not exaggerate the lot of this majority: "My house is so rotten you can jest take up the boards in your hands and cromple 'em up. Everything done swunk about it."

Although living on abundant land in the south temperate zone, tenant families have probably the most meager and ill-balanced diet of any large group in America. Devotion to the single cash-crop, and the fact that food crops mature during the same season as cotton, make it virtually impossible under the system to raise subsistence crops. Because the growing of household produce does not fit into the economy of a cash-crop, it is not encouraged by landlords, whose prerogative it is to determine the crops grown. As a result the diet is limited largely to imported foods, made available through the commissaries and local stores. This diet can be, and commonly is, strained down to the notorious three M's,—meat (fat salt pork), meal, and molasses. Evidence of the slow ravages of this diet are to be found in the widespread incidence of pellagra, which Dr. Joseph Goldberger of the United States Public Health Service bluntly attributes to lack of proper food. This diet is a part of the very culture of tenancy, supported by habit, convenience, and cheapness. A dietary survey reported by Rupert B. Vance revealed significantly that the maize kernel constituted 23 per cent of the total food intake of white Tennessee and Georgia mountaineers, 32.5 per cent of that of southern Negroes, chiefly tenant farmers, but only 1.6 per cent of that of northern families in comfortable circumstances. Pork—chiefly fat salt pork—makes up 40 per cent of the food of southern tenant farmers.

Food is the largest item in the tenant's budget, and since almost no food is produced, it must be purchased. In six counties, the average monthly expenditure for food in 1934 was $12.34, or about $3.08 per week for the average family of five. As small as these amounts seem, they consume the major portion of the tenant's income.

FURNISHING

The current credit used by share tenants is commonly known as "furnishing." The landlord furnishes his tenants with food and other necessities during the crop production period and is paid for these advances out of the tenants' share of the crop in the settlement at harvest time. The usual rationing consists of furnishing groceries from the commissary to a tenant and his family. The tenant does not know the money value of what he is receiving or, to be more exact, he does not know what he is being charged for it. Variations of furnishing are the less frequently used "account" from which the tenant makes purchases with some knowledge of what he is being charged, and the "limit," whereby the landlord allows the tenant commodities up to some fixed amount.

Under the "rations" system the tenant receives little, and often suffers rank exploitation. In some instances large plantations allot to each laborer two pecks of meal and four pounds of fat back pork every two weeks. Some of the landlords are even more niggardly, providing tenants only meal and leaving them to provide meat as best they can. The testimony of tenants, supported by the observation of bare cupboards, points to extreme meagerness.

> We can't get any flour, snuff, shoes, sugar, coffee, thread or anything from the landlord but meat and meal. We have a divil of a time. No soap, soda, or salt. Can't borrow a dime, not a damn cent. If this ain't hell, I'll eat you. We work our damn heads off and git nothing. The harder we work, the deeper in debt we gits.

The restriction of the landlord's advance does not, however, prevent a heavy debt at the close of the year.

> Boss said after we's gathered the crop last year, I still owed him $130.00. Sometimes we got less than 15 pounds of meat and two bushels of meal every two weeks.

A Negro woman reported her conversation with her landlord, about furnishing, and his sympathetic response:

> Yesterday, Mr. ——, the boss man, come through the field and asked me how I feel. I just stopped my hoeing and said, "Mr. ——, I just don't know how I feel." He says, "What's the trouble, Julia, don't you feel well?" I say, "I'm just hungry, Mr. ——." "Ain't you got nothing to eat at your house, Julia?" "I ain't got nothing but fat back and corn bread, and I done eat that so long that I believe I got the pellagacy, Mr. ——." His face turns red when I say that, and he said, "Well, Saturday I'm gonna give you some flour too. Just come by the office."

The amounts allowed tenants under the several systems of furnishing and the period over which the credit extends are determined by the landlord. The "margin of progress" possible to the tenant is generally so small that he is constantly dependent upon credit at any terms. The amounts croppers receive are not sufficient for a family by any standard of adequacy. The fact that millions live and work under these conditions offers little ground for national pride when death and sickness rates are included in the picture.

No Incentive to Improvement

Since the tenant has no legal claims on any improvements he may make, he has no interest in conserving or improving either the land or the buildings. On the contrary, just as it is to his advantage to rob the soil of its fertility, so he is tempted to burn for firewood rails from any nearby fence or planks from the porch floor or from an outhouse—if the place happens to be distinguished by having any movable materials that have not already succumbed to the ravages of time and tenants. The tenant is not likely to trouble to make any repairs that are not absolutely necessary, and these few will be so made as not to outlast his stay on the place.

Under a system which does not encourage labor and thrift men easily develop habits of improvidence. As matters now stand, the tenant who really works on his place, who labors to restore the soil, who repairs and builds, is merely inviting his landlord to raise his rent. If he should use all his time and energy in improving the place on which he lives, with the hope of ultimately raising his own status, the tenant would have no recourse if his landlord demanded a higher rent or notified him that he would have to leave the next year. It may

be argued that landlords generally would not follow
any such course; but the absence of any laws on the
statute books of the southern states protecting tenants
in improvements made by them is a final answer to such
arguments. Those who say that legal protection for the
tenant is unnecessary, that we have too many laws, will
have difficulty in justifying the crop lien laws which
protect the immediate interests of the merchants and
landlords, but ignore the immediate interests of the
tenants and the long-time interests of every one in the
region.

Is it any wonder, then, that the soil is exhausted,
buildings not fit for habitation, and the tenants themselves thoroughly inured to habits and attitudes that, if
undisturbed, will keep them impoverished? There can
be no general prosperity among any class for long in
such an environment.

What the Status of Tenancy Means

It is a notorious and shameful fact that the stock
arguments employed against any serious efforts to improve the lot of the cotton tenant are based upon the
very social and cultural conditions which tenancy itself
creates. The mobility of the tenant, his dependence,
his lack of ambition, shiftlessness, his ignorance and
poverty, the lethargy of his pellagra-ridden body, provide a ready excuse for keeping him under a stern
paternalistic control. There is not a single trait alleged

which, where true, does not owe its source and continuance to the imposed status itself.

The status of tenancy demands complete dependence; it requires no education and demands no initiative, since the landlord assumes the prerogative of direction in the choice of crop, the method by which it shall be cultivated, and how and when and where it shall be sold. He keeps the records and determines the earnings. Through the commissary or credit merchant, even the choice of diet is determined. The landlord can determine the kind and amount of schooling for the children, the extent to which they may share benefits intended for all the people. He may even determine the relief they receive in the extremity of their distress. He controls the courts, the agencies of law enforcement and, as in the case of share-croppers in eastern Arkansas, can effectively thwart any efforts at organization to protect their meager rights.

The present system is so constructed that the landless remain landless and the propertyless remain propertyless. To accumulate property, to increase independence, is to oppose the system itself. In a plantation area it is easier to be a cropper and conform to the system than to be a small owner or renter. For a share tenant to rise above his status he must overcome insuperable obstacles: (1) the agriculture that he knows fits only the old system, (2) the banks cannot finance him because they are geared to finance the plantations, (3) the cost of merchant credit dissipates his accumulated working capital, and (4) the crop lien credit system has destroyed his independence in the marketing of his crop.

Neither ambition, nor thrift, nor self-respect can thrive in such a climate. Not only is it impossible to develop a hardy stock of ambitious farm owners—the persistent American ideal—but it is impossible to avoid physical and moral decadence.

If the tenant is lazy, this is a result of his mode of life. As a Mississippian, H. Snyder, writing candidly in the *North American Review*, observes: "Certainly the common run of people in the South are poor, and we are told this poverty is born of their laziness. But this is upside down, as their laziness is born of their poverty."

Attempts to justify the existing system of tenure on the score that it is an adaptation to the latent and innate characteristics and capacities of the southern farm population are as baseless as they are vicious. All such observable characteristics can be traced directly to the system of tenure and the mode of livelihood that it promotes. The system, says Arthur N. Moore of the Georgia Experiment Station, does not provide ". . . a friendly atmosphere for the development of latent capacities."

Such in brief detail is the life of the tenant—drear, meager, and changeless. Upon this is reared an agricultural system which custom and a temporary federal subsidy are holding together against the insistent need of complete reorganization.

Let us now look for a moment at certain other central features of the industry of cotton culture.

II

A PRECARIOUS CREDIT SYSTEM

LOUIS XIV of France observed with a grim irony that "credit supports agriculture, as the cord supports the hanged." For sixty years cotton culture has been strangling under an impossible system of finance. Only a very favorable world market for this staple has permitted survival of the system and the complex of social institutions bound up with it. Now, with the great and growing competition of other cotton-growing areas in the world, and newer problems of production and consumption, the cotton system faces finally and perhaps fatally the consequences of unsound credit.

Even under slavery the chief capital supporting cotton cultivation was not available in the South, a situation which kept the whole area in a secondary slavery to the capital of the North. In 1850 when the total cotton, rice, and sugar sales amounted to $119,400,000, the total bank deposits in the South were around $20,000,000. In 1860 when the value of crops reached $200,000,000, less than $30,000,000 was in southern banks. There has been a continuing lack of short-term credit to finance annual operations, for both productive and consumptive purposes. Bank credit in the South has been inadequate, and this has made necessary reliance upon other and costly sources.

In the cotton belt there is a high seasonality of both agricultural loans and bank deposits. The volume of loans is highest at precisely the time when deposits are lowest. In a one-crop system the bulk of farm income is in the fall and early winter months. The need for loans is in the spring and summer. Since cash deposits provide the body of lendable funds, it is impossible to meet demands of farmers for current financing, and, at the same time, maintain adequate reserves for safety.

Most loans on cotton crops are essentially speculative and this risk increases their cost. The hierarchy of these loans, with risk and service charges, results in an insupportable accumulation of credit costs for the groups lowest down. The credit merchant becomes an almost inescapable part of the credit structure, and is a response to the erratic nature of farm income under the exclusive one-crop economy. These credit costs, on the basis of studies made by the Department of Agriculture, have been shown to drain off 25 to 50 per cent from the operating capital of the small dependent farmers.

The three most important sources of credit for the small farmer in the South, before introduction of the federal credit agencies, have been (1) the landlords,

(2) the merchants and dealers, and (3) the local commercial banks. The high cost of merchant and landlord credit, when this includes both the tangible and intangible costs, has been a retarding factor in the progress of the tenant and small owner classes of both white and Negro farmers. A mortgage or lien on the crop is regularly given as security. This gives the creditor domination over the debtor and final control of the cotton crop. As long as the crop lien is given as security for a loan and all financing is done through the agency which holds this crop lien, there is little chance of improvement in the short-time credit conditions of farmers.

There is little hope of any economic progress for the tenant farmer generally, under the old credit system. What has actually happened is that the landlord and credit merchant, instead of promoting advancement in agricultural and social development, have been financing economic stagnation and backwardness. Where credit costs cut out the *margin of progress*, or the small accumulations by which ownership is eventually acquired, there can be no economic growth.

The Credit Merchant

Closest to the share tenant and cropper is the credit merchant. He may be a merchant only or he may be a landlord controlling the business, not only of his own tenants, but of any other renters and small owners who need to be "furnished." Through his own farming operations he can secure from one-half to two-thirds of the tenants' productivity, and through his commercial operations he can, and often does, secure the rest. As the system is at present organized he is essential to his own tenants and to croppers and share tenants on the plantations of absentee and non-furnishing landlords. In such a position he can and often does exact a high and exhausting tribute. He justifies his interest charges and time prices on the ground of risk. The method in practice, thus, is to sell on credit to the farmer "all that the trade can carry" and charge as much as the borrower can bear.

The credit merchant's security is the entire crop, which when harvested and ginned, must be turned over for disposal by the creditor in payment of the debt. The merchant keeps the books and sets the interest and time prices. Even if the merchant is fair and does not charge exorbitant prices and extortionate interest, there may be no balance or there may be a debt for the tenant. In any case, the tenant rarely if ever gets a detailed statement of his debits and credits. He has no choice but to accept the settlement given him. In earlier times the prestige of the white merchant or planter forbade any questioning of the account by the Negro tenant; today the prestige of the established credit system forbids questioning of accounts by either black or white tenants. Sentiment can play but small part in such a system and where "reasonable profits" mean bare subsistence for the workers, few favors and no questioning can be indulged. These merchants, when they are candid with themselves, see the viciousness of the system of which they are a part. One justification is that the excesses are necessary for survival in competition on a low level. A South Carolina merchant, who had changed his own practices and abandoned the prevailing customs, said:

We used to do a general credit business carrying many accounts. We charged interest plus a time price which amounted to 50 per cent. Thirty per cent was supposed to cover costs of operating the store, and supervision of farms, and 20 per cent was supposed to cover losses on accounts. We went bankrupt on this basis and changed our practice when my brother and I started this store. We now select very carefully those tenants that we "furnish" and charge them only a flat rate of 10 per cent which is assessed upon the account as it stands on September 30th.

I think the old credit system is wrong. Any system of "furnishing" which expects a 20 per cent loss is wrong. The old system is extortionate and too great a burden for the farmer to bear. We pick our risks and try to deal fairly with them. You won't find this a general practice.

This statement illustrates clearly the dilemma facing every one who lives in the region. The merchant who chooses his risks carefully can abandon the prevailing customs. But what would happen if all merchants did this? Who would take the chances on the bad risks? We can be sure that no other agency could take the same chances of loss on a purely commercial basis without at the same time exacting the same terms and securing the same chances for profit. There is no reason to believe any other commercial agency would do this better than it is now done.

Because of the prevailing customs, the merchant or planter may exact exorbitant charges without feeling that any injustice is being done the tenant. It is possible to avoid the laws regulating interest charges by levying service charges and management costs. As one planter bluntly stated:

> There are more ways of whipping the devil than around the stump. We don't charge interest. We charge a 25 per cent manager's fee, that pays for the rider, manager service, and supervision costs.

Even where a merchant wants to be fair to his tenants he is promptly placed at a disadvantage in competition with less scrupulous ones. A south Texas merchant complained about a group of competitors:

> They advance a man cash or furnishings and in most cases they tie the man up so he never pays out of debt, which keeps the farmer forever using the fur-

nishings of their stores. There are all sorts of unfair-
ness in this type of business. A tenant of mine came to
me and said that —— promised that he would give
him a certain price for his cotton on payment of his
account. When the cotton was delivered —— had reduced the price to another figure.... That shows you
just how tenants are cheated out of their incomes and
are kept perpetually in debt.

It is not that merchants are always cruel to their
tenants. A common figure in the cotton belt is the paternalistic planter-merchant who renders kindly services
and is in turn the only person of influence to whom
dependents can turn in distress. The seriousness and
tragedy of the situation lie in the fact that the merchant
is virtually forced to exploit the tenant if he is himself
to survive. For the credit merchant and the planter himself are in turn supported by the commercial banking
system. And although merchants and landlords may
even help to control the banks, banking capital is scarce
because the masses of the people have little savings. The
bulk of the savings among the rural population belongs
to the landlords, and this is not enough.

The simple per annum interest rates in 1934 in three
selected cotton counties studied in Mississippi and
Texas, varied from 16.1 per cent to 25.3 per cent. In
addition to this, however, were credit prices. In these
same communities the excess of the credit price was
found to be greater even than the interest charges, and

the total cost to the tenant for his supplies averaged more than 50 per cent per annum.

With a systematic charge of 50 per cent for production and consumption credit, the tenant fails to accumulate capital or even to get out of debt; and the small farm-owner is in constant danger of falling into the tenant class. The census figures on the startling increase in tenancy indicate that this is exactly what is happening.

CONCENTRATION OF LAND OWNERSHIP

The outcome of the precarious credit structure which seems to have escaped general attention, is the quiet concentration of land in impersonal ownership. The Civil War and the following period of disorganization of southern agriculture witnessed a progressive breaking up of many large cotton plantations into small holdings. This trend continued until the decade of the 80's. With the turn of the century, conditions changed. The South now is experiencing a re-concentration of tenant farms under corporate ownership. In 1900 the census of agriculture shows the number of rented farms possessed by landlords owning five or more rented farms in Mississippi as 53.1 per cent. In 1920 the Bureau of Agricultural Economics found, in a study of five selected areas of the Mississippi Delta, that 81.2 per cent of the rented farms were so possessed. Although the areas are not strictly comparable, similar differences are found in other states between 1900 and 1920, when compared with the selected areas studied by the Bureau of Agricultural Economics. Such indications led Dr. Rupert Vance to conclude that "even before the disasters of 1920-1925 the trend toward land concentration was resumed." It is estimated that areas amounting to 30 per cent of the cotton lands of various states are owned by insurance companies and banks.

It is apparent that during times of normal prosperity in the cotton planting industry, since about 1880, the better lands of the South have been progressively concentrated into large plantations under central management. Many of these plantations have fallen into the hands of large creditor institutions, and at the present time enormous holdings are in the hands of a few of these institutions. Whether or not this concentration will continue, will depend upon the future prices of cotton, the continued profitableness of the plantation type of farm organization, the success of plantation owners in liquidating the present mortgage indebtedness without dissolution, and the ability of others to recover property they have lost. But whatever view one takes of the system, it is certain that it has not operated to the benefit of those living under it, and future prospects, unless the system is altered, are even darker than the past. In the past the tenant has paid with his labor and his life; later the landlord has paid with his land and his capital.

III

IS KING COTTON
DOOMED?

THE weight of tradition and memories of grandeur and opulence now forever gone are in sharp conflict with new economic realities. When the cotton kingdom reached its apogee, around the middle of the 19th century, there were contributing factors of a highly favorable character. Before the development of an efficient gin the whole civilized world had been awaiting a cheap textile as a substitute for the expensive woolens, silks, and linens. There was an eager world market based upon an almost universal clothing need. The United States was the chief cotton producing country in the world. In the South it had the soil, the climate and vast areas of cotton lands for expansion and exploitation. In the absence of perfected machinery for picking there was an army of controlled black labor, profitable for use only with such a staple crop. The vast possibilities of wealth gave permanence to the one-crop economy, prevented a balanced agriculture because it was not then needed, and in the end thwarted the growth of other agricultural skills.

Today every factor found so favorable in the earlier period is profoundly changed, although hope springs eternal for the return of the old days. Cotton will probably remain for many years the principal cash crop of the South, for this area still has one of the best climates in the world and most favorable natural conditions for production. But the old plantation type of farm organization, the one-crop pattern, the system of tenure, of finance and production, are of an unreclaimable past. They must be changed entirely if the best interests of the area are to be promoted—if the system itself is to escape dismal collapse.

Loss of Soil Fertility

One of the major indictments of the one-crop system is that it encourages waste and improvidence on the part of both landlord and tenant. Constant cropping without thought of permanently maintaining the fertility of the soil has seriously reduced the possibility, for a long time to come, of low cost cotton production under any type of farm organization in all except a few favored regions of the Old South. The introduction of livestock and other methods of soil improvement is a long and tedious matter. Yet this must be done if the soil of the Old South is to be revitalized. Under any circumstance, restoration of the soil will necessitate a radical change in the farming system, and the permanent reduction of acreage put to cotton. While this is going on, it is not unlikely that the newer south-western areas will be forging ahead in commercial cotton production and repeating the errors of the South-east.

The speculative spirit which is so characteristic of the whole system of cotton production was fostered in the beginning by a wasteful land policy. In the plow and sickle age, the 1,465,000,000 acres of government land seemed inexhaustible, and it was solemnly reported by the Secretary of the Treasury in 1827 that it would take no less than 500 years to settle the public domain. The whole thought was that of appropriation and reckless utilization. But where are the lands today? A quarter of a century ago the end of the frontier was reached, with millions of acres of ruined and useless cotton land left behind to feed only the recurring hopes of impoverished farmers.

Loss of World Markets

The problem of the cotton surplus was one of the first to engage the efforts of the government in its recent desperate recovery attempts. It was with the thought of restoring collapsed prices that drastic acreage reduction was demanded. The irony of half-clothed field workers destroying cotton because they were unable to buy it, is now an old, if unpleasant, memory.

One cause of this surplus has been the decline in world markets. At one time the one great producer of this staple for world consumption, the United States today is one of fifty cotton-growing countries in the world. For years Indian crops have been developing successfully as a substitute for American cotton. Egypt produces the best cotton grown in the world. Brazil is well adapted to cotton cultivation and has an even larger available acreage than the United States. Great Britain has been encouraging the cultivation of this crop in its colonies, and has materially increased this development through careful research and stimulation. Nigeria, Uganda, the Sudan, Nyasaland, and Rhodesia are new cotton-growing countries, and are capable of large production, as are Persia, Australia, and Syria. Japan and China are providing increasing amounts for their own consumption, and Japan is promoting cotton culture in countries of the East over which it has hegemony. Russia has recently dropped out of the market as a buyer, being able to supply her own needs. Later she may be able to export a surplus. In 1921, for example, Russian cotton production was a bare 43,000 bales; in 1932-33 it had jumped to 1,800,000 bales.

Increased foreign demand will depend both upon increased industrial activity abroad, and upon the removal of international trade restrictions. The problem of tariff reduction is too complicated and forbidding both at home and abroad to offer much hope. For even if the United States holds a dominant position it cannot control prices, and any amount of stocks from foreign sources will be sufficient to "spoil" the price.

Professor John A. Todd, the foremost authority on the world's cotton crops, makes this disconcerting observation:

> In all this discussion of cotton growing throughout the world there is one common feature which is of paramount importance to America. Not only are the world's supplies other than American increasing steadily, if slowly, in quantity, but also the great bulk of the new supplies is of a quality at least as good as all but the best American, and every one of the countries mentioned is doing what it can to produce the best cotton it is capable of growing, or to improve the varieties formerly grown. Contrast this with the position in America where the history of the last 20 years has been one of almost steady deterioration in the average quality of the crop.

UNCERTAIN AND PESSIMISTIC OUTLOOK FOR COTTON PRICES

Cotton prices are among the most erratic and fluctuating of all agricultural markets. They show an unusual sensitiveness to general conditions of demand and to the conditions of both the domestic and world supplies of the crop. These extreme fluctuations have been a constant source of harassment and instability for the fixed and unwieldy one-crop system around which southern farms have been organized. The violence and frequency of cotton price fluctuations have increased since the World War.

It is significant that, since the drastic reduction in American production beginning in 1932, there has been a directly compensating increase in cotton growing abroad. During the years of intense depression (1930-1932) the world consumption of other than American cotton reached the highest level in history. The price and consumption problem has been further complicated by the international debt situation. The United States, since the war, has for the first time in history found itself a great creditor nation. The debtor nations of Europe, until the collapse of all effort at payment, were forced to reduce imports from America to as low a point as possible and export to America as much as they could. The most optimistic now have ceased to expect a return to price levels of the post-war years of 1923 to 1925 when profits, for a brief period, revived the weakening structure, giving it the illusory aspect of a new and vigorous institution.

Low-Cost Production in the Southwest

The center of cotton production has been constantly moving westward. Before 1850 the bulk of the cotton was produced in the Carolinas, Georgia, Alabama, and Mississippi. Now Mississippi and the states west of the Mississippi River produce nearly three-fourths of the

United States total. Texas and Oklahoma alone produce nearly one-half.

The potential development of cotton lands in the Southwest is indicated by the rapid increase in Texas and Oklahoma acreages between 1919 and 1929; that is, before the present depression set in. During this period Texas added 7,024,000 acres in cotton and Oklahoma added 1,851,000 acres. Given necessary impetus, Texas could expand in cotton acreage considerably.

The present situation, in a ten-year average for the period 1923-32, is as follows:

The world consumption of American cotton	13,377,900 bales
Domestic consumption of American cotton	5,959,200 "
The production of cotton in Mississippi and states west of the Mississippi River	9,079,300 "
The production of cotton in remaining states	4,298,600 "
Production of cotton in Texas and Oklahoma	5,860,000 "

If the trend continues, Mississippi and the states west of the Mississippi River can easily supply the world consumption of American cotton, leaving a vast population in the eastern South stranded completely.

In certain of these West Texas areas the cost of production has been reduced to a point where farmers can raise cotton profitably at a price of six cents a pound. The spread of mechanization will probably cause expansion of cotton production in these new areas. The competition of these areas further darkens the price outlook for cotton in the Old South. Even the availability of cheap commercial fertilizer could not avert the rapid development of mechanized farms in the Southwest, unless there is serious reorganization of farming in the Old South.

MECHANIZATION OF FARMING

One characteristic of cotton production has been the continued use of small implements and hand labor. Rapid progress has been made in the adapting of machinery to agriculture generally. Increased demand for low-cost production has made this necessary. Cotton production has been last to attempt mechanization, but is coming to it now with surprising vigor in the newer cotton areas. Neither the old plantation organization nor the simple one-horse farm has been, in the past, adaptable to the use of machinery. What seems at present imminent is that the Southwest, which is better adapted to the use of machinery, will continue to increase the use of it.

The tractor and the two row equipment lower the man labor requirements per acre. Where these machines are used the size of the average cotton farm is increasing. In the old cotton area of the Southeast, the average area cultivated was 10 to 20 acres by a family with one mule and plow. In the western area the average family can handle from 100 to 150 acres, using two row equipment drawn by four or six mules. The tractors increase this acreage even more. The lowered operating costs under machinery can best be shown in the figures from one Delta experiment station at Stoneville, Mississippi, reported by P. H. Stephens in his paper, "Mechanization of Cotton Farms."

OPERATING COSTS PER ACRE OF COTTON AT THE DELTA
EXPERIMENT STATION, STONEVILLE, MISSISSIPPI

Equipment	Power	Labor, power and machinery cost per acre
½ row	One mule	$14.20
1 row walking	Two mules	11.19
1 row riding	Two mules	10.78
2 row	Four mules	8.97
2 row	Tractor	6.78
4 row	Tractor	5.20

Men cannot possibly compete with machines in such a system as now exists and maintain a satisfactory standard of living. The barriers to the introduction of machinery in the Southeast have been the topography

and the plantation system itself. These are very largely
overcome in the Southwest.

As Dr. A. B. Conner, the director of the Texas Experiment Station, said:

> The man in the bottoms can't compete with the
> western cotton farmer who can produce cotton for six
> cents a pound. The old system of tenantry is doomed,
> I believe. The best thing for the tenant is to jump in
> and become a machinery operator. Two years ago I
> was talking to Ward Templeman down at Navasota.
> He sold all his mules and bought tractors. He just put
> it up to them and told them the best tractor operators
> would get the jobs. They proved to be able operators.
> He said his best tractor operators on his place were
> his tenants. That's what I would advise tenants. When
> they begin using machinery go to the landlord and tell
> him you want a job as a machine operator.   They can
> do it. There's no saying that they can't do it. The
> model T Ford has given them a liberal education on
> machinery. This man in the bottoms is not mistreating
> the tenants as much as he is trying to survive for eco-
> nomic necessity. He's got to reduce his production
> costs to allow him to compete with the man who can
> produce it cheaper in West Texas. Out there with
> machinery one man can handle two hundred acres of
> land.

There is impending a violent revolution in cotton
production as a result of the development of the me-

chanical cotton picker. Cotton has awaited this event
with the eagerness that it awaited the development of
the gin. When it comes it will automatically release
hundreds of thousands of cotton workers particularly
in the Southeast, creating a new range of social problems. The International Harvester Company is reported
to have spent some $3,000,000 experimenting with this
device. Types have been developed which have proved
fairly successful, although too expensive for small-scale
use. Within the past two years, however, there has
been successfully tried out, at the Delta Experiment
Station in Mississippi, a mechanical cotton picker capable of doing in seven and a half hours, the work of
three and a half months of a good hand picker. It is not
expected that sentiment or public policy can prevent its
use merely on the grounds that it will displace workers.
This is the course of machinery in every field.

The Competition of Other Fabrics

The old position of cotton is menaced by factors
other than competing cotton areas. Rayon is the most
formidable of these new competitors. The industry began comparatively recently, but is now our third largest
textile. At first the industry was confined largely to
Europe, where it made considerable progress. Then
rayon began to be manufactured in the United States
on a very limited scale. In 1910 the first great plant
was constructed in this country, and by 1912 the con-

sumption of rayon was 2,700,000 pounds of which 59
per cent was imported. In 1923 the United States consumption was 39,400,000 pounds of which only 10
per cent was imported. Since the war the growth of
the industry has been rapid, and this growth has been
a direct response to an increased demand which reflects
its inroads on cotton as a dress fabric. In addition to
rayon other synthetic fabrics, which can be cheaply
manufactured, are preferred to cotton for many types
of wearing apparel and are gaining ground with men-
acing rapidity.

IV

THE COTTON TENANT UNDER THE
DEPRESSION AND RECOVERY
PROGRAMS

CONDITIONS in the Cotton Belt needed but the
impact of the world-wide depression to become intol-
erable to bankers, landlords, small owners and tenants
alike. War and post-war conditions served finally to
upset whatever fluctuating balance the Cotton Belt had
been able to attain between the forces of supply and
world demand. The price of cotton under war demands
reached a new high in 1918 though a corresponding
increase in production was delayed for several years
by the severe ravages of the boll weevil which in 1929
was estimated to have reduced the crop by 30 per cent.
After a brief post-war slump prices recovered, the in-
centive to production taught new forms of weevil control, and acreage was extended in the Mississippi Valley
and the northern and western fringes farthest removed
from the insect's depredations.

What Georgia, South Carolina, and Alabama lost,
Texas and Oklahoma more than regained in cotton acres
and cotton bales. From 1921 to 1926 Texas placed seven
million new acres in cotton cultivation while in the

same period the United States' total increased from thirty million to forty-six million acres. Under the influence of high prices and subsidies, foreign production kept pace with American, so that by 1928 signs of price breaks indicated that production had been pushed too far. With the emergence of world depression, consumption fell sharply and the carry-over of the American crop in the period 1929-30 to 1932-33 increased from five million to thirteen million bales. The effect of the down-swing on the Cotton Belt was nothing less than a major disaster. From 1928-29 to 1932-33 the gross farm income from cotton and cotton seed fell from $1,470,000,000 to $431,000,000, with the result that the average gross income per farm family engaged in cotton growing fell from $735 to $216. At its new low point in June, 1932, the average farm price of cotton stood at 4.6 cents per pound. Economic distress and actual misery prevailed in practically every section of the Belt, falling most heavily on tenants and croppers many of whom, reduced below subsistence levels, were forced on public relief. The year's production added to the carry-over, amounted to twenty-six million bales of American cotton alone, a fact which promised no respite from the crushing burdens faced by the South.

The Crop Reduction Program

Such, in brief, is the course of events which forced individualistic cotton farmers to the acceptance of, if not the insistence on, federal regimentation. It is noteworthy that the first use of state compulsion to reduce cotton acreage was sponsored by a recent governor of Louisiana, a folk product who lives with his ear to the ground. The legislation passed by Louisiana, Texas, and South Carolina in the fall and winter of 1931-32, thwarted though it was by our peculiar federal structure and by the folk themselves, nevertheless indicated the South's demand for some form of acreage control. Once the allotment plan was agreed upon, the plow-up campaign and the 1934 acreage reduction followed as a matter of course. The Bankhead Bill can be regarded largely as an attempt of the cotton grower to reach by legal penalties his recalcitrant neighbors who refused to sign acreage reduction contracts for 1934.

The Agricultural Adjustment Administration was created "to relieve the existing national economic emergency by increasing agricultural purchasing power." The adoption in the spring of 1933 of the Domestic Allotment plan with rental and parity payments to those who voluntarily reduced their acreage found the cotton crop already planted. Unless another large crop was to be added to the crushing burden of the surplus, drastic measures were a necessity. They were undertaken in the plow-up campaign which is estimated to have taken 10,400,000 acres and 4,400,000 bales out of production. By contracts with the Secretary of Agriculture producers obligated themselves to plow

up between 25 and 50 per cent of their acreage for
which they were to receive a rental payment of approximately $11 per acre, depending upon the per acre
yields. The producer might take his payment all in
cash or part in options on cotton formerly held by the
Farm Board. The 1933 crop, in spite of an estimated
plow-up of 4,400,000 bales, amounted to about 13,200,-
000 bales. This gave a carry-over of 10,000,000 bales
which was a reduction of only 1,000,000 bales from
the year before.

For landowners there is no doubt that the program
was a success. The price of cotton went to ten cents
where it was pegged by government loans. Crop re-
ceipts plus benefit payments gave the growers more than
double the income of the previous year 1932.

Through December 31, 1933, the AAA distributed
$111,405,244.37 in rental and benefit payments in the
cotton plow-up campaign. This was 85.6 per cent of
the total amount spent in rental and benefit payments
and 63.9 per cent of the total sum, $175,404,851.64
spent for both rental and benefits and the removal of
surplus in cotton, wheat, tobacco, hogs, and butter.
The South absorbed approximately 85.5 per cent of
these payments. Many of the great Delta counties with
90 per cent tenancy and high Negro ratios received
from $500,000 to over $800,000 in benefit payments
alone. With white landowners, who own most of the
plantations, comprising about 2 per cent of all farm

operators, it remains a moot question as to how evenly these benefits were distributed among the tenants. The question is all the more important because the tenants had tilled the crops until the plow-up and thus possessed an equity in the destroyed crops.

The government under the AAA has assumed many of the risks of the landowners, and thrown them on the tenant. The risk of overproduction is met by fixed quotas with rent to the landowner for his retired lands. These benefits take little, if any, account of labor's previous interest in the crop. The tenant's share of rental is pitifully small or nil, and on him is thrown the brunt of reduced acreage. The risk of price fluctuation is met by the government's policy of pegging prices by loans at, say, ten cents per pound on cotton. Through its production credit corporations the Federal Farm Credit Administration offers the landowner production credit at $4\frac{1}{2}$ to $6\frac{1}{2}$ per cent interest. The tenant cannot secure this cheap credit unless the landlord waives his first lien on the crop. If the tenant does not agree to release his share of the crop lien to the governmental agency, the landlord may then secure the loan for all his tenant farms at $4\frac{1}{2}$ to $6\frac{1}{2}$ per cent and then advance supplies and furnishings to his tenants at customary credit prices, 20 to 30 per cent above cash prices. Here again the tenant bears the brunt of the credit; if he cannot repay, he loses his crop and whatever chattel and work-stock he may possess.

The risk of losing equity in farms has been lessened for owners by methods of refinancing through the Farm Credit Administration and by arrangements for scaling down debts in conference with creditors. So far the various Debt Reconciliation Commissions have made no attempts to have landlords scale down debts owed them from previous seasons by croppers and share tenants. Such proposals would be resented, no doubt, by landowners although they had just had their own debts scaled down by creditors. There is a New Testament parable on this subject, but the quoting of Scripture in economic treatises has never gained much vogue.

It is but the blunt truth to say that under the present system the landowner is more and more protected from risk by government activity, while the tenant is left open to risks on every side. Only after he loses first what property he may possess and then his tenure, does the tenant come to the form of risk insurance designed for him—relief.

One obvious reason for the wholesale neglect of the tenant lies in the fact that the Agricultural Adjustment Administration organized its program under the direction of the planters themselves. When suddenly curtailment of production was ordered the law was obeyed but the customary tenant-landlord relations managed to persist. Planters found that the indemnity for reduction supplied greatly needed cash. Since most of the money allocated to the South came to them, the program did not seem entirely unsatisfactory. The AAA as finally administered met the landlord's approval. If it effected any disorganization, that disorganization was not inimical to the planters' interest. Ultimately it proved to be merely a subsidy to planters.

The field studies of the Committee indicate that, in practice, the landlord's reduction was the farm quota and he determined the distribution of the reduced acreage among his tenants. The share-croppers seldom received cash as payment for their reduction. For the most part landlords "credited to their accounts" the amounts due them. The participation of tenants in the reduction program was not general. Many tenants were not required to reduce their acreages if the plantation had held within its quota. In some instances the county quota was filled without requiring a reduction on certain farms. Those who plowed up no cotton, of course, received aid only in the form of higher prices for their product. Some who did plow up received nothing.

In Bolivar County, Mississippi, many large plantations reduced the "wage hand crop"—that is, the land cultivated by the owner with hired labor—and did not disturb the tenant crops. In Marlboro County, South Carolina, the same practice held. A cropper commented, "Our landlord wouldn't plow up any of our cotton. He plowed up his own so that he could get the pay for it." In Fort Bend County, Texas, the county quota was filled before small farmers were taken in.

Greatest participation in the benefits of reduction was found in the areas where cotton farming was least profitable. In Bolivar County, Mississippi, a productive area, 47 per cent of those reducing cotton acreage received cash payments. In Marlboro County, South Carolina, a poorer county, all of the tenants plowing up received some cash. In Harrison and Fort Bend Counties in Texas the numbers receiving cash for cotton reduction were 87.5 per cent and 85.8 per cent respectively. It would, perhaps, be more accurate to say that these tenants were credited by the government with receiving cash. In many cases the cash was promptly applied against the indebtedness of the tenant to the owners. In Bolivar County, Mississippi, a half-cropper said: "I plowed up six acres of my cotton last year, but I didn't get a cent from the government. Boss said it was credited to my account, but I don't know." This tenant was not familiar with the amount of his indebtedness or the amount applied to his debts. Another tenant, however, was better informed. "When I plowed up my cotton I got $136.00 deducted from my account. It was really deducted, for I saw the statement itemized." In some instances tenants were allowed a small part of the money due them in cash. A half-cropper plowed up five acres of cotton and got $11.00 cash. The remainder was credited to his account.

In Harrison County, Texas, where the small farm and credit merchant predominate, the system of crediting accounts could not be used, but a system was developed which was equally as effective in preventing tenants from securing the cash.

> Mr. —— and the others brought the checks out here to the store and that's where we signed up. The merchant taken them and give credit for them. Some of the folks got a little something out of theirs but I just signed mine and give it to him. I asked him for some of mine back and he said "nothing doing." I didn't want to act hard cause I know it wouldn't get me nowheres.

The county agents in charge of distribution of the payment made the credit stores points for distributing checks. As a result checks were passed over to merchants either for unpaid debts or for future supplies. In many cases the merchant suggested that the checks be given him and that he would furnish the given farmer until his check was consumed. Such a suggestion is practically an edict under the prevailing relationships in the rural South.

In all areas, the benefits of reduction accrued ultimately to the landlord and merchant. A farmer in Noxubee County, Mississippi, when asked about the federal payments said with bitter humor: "It's been here, oh, it's been here. More of the bosses have redeemed homes and redeemed their lands and bought cars in Noxubee

County than they did during the World War, and the poor people have suffered more."

In spite of the best intentions of the Washington administration, the 1933 crop reduction program was handled clumsily. Some tenants plowed up cotton; some did not. Those who received payment in cash did not receive the same amount for the same acreage. There was considerable confusion in the tenants' participation. The 1934 program found the dominating forces better organized, the tenants more carefully avoided in the administration of the relief program. The acreage quotas were determined and the landowner rented acres to the Secretary of Agriculture and the only information given the tenant was that he could plant a stipulated amount of cotton.

The code for cotton production has been properly designated "the landlord's code" and all that was not provided to the landlord's satisfaction in the code was taken care of in the administration of it. Many tenants actually paid for use of land rented to the Secretary of Agriculture and specified as available for planting food crops rent free.

The tenant found himself the loser in any event; if he was not displaced from the farm entirely, he remained as a casual laborer, and if he did not suffer this change in status, his operations were so small as to be unprofitable. The organization of the national machinery provided representation to adjust difficulties in the administration of the program, but it was not found possible to give personal attention to all complaints registered. Complaints sent to the Department of Agriculture in Washington were sent to state AAA administrators for adjustment, where they were passed to county agents for adjustment. These agents in turn passed them to the landlord against whom the complaint was made. A complaint often ended in further injury and discomfiture to the complainant.

The planters organized and the first Bankhead Bill dovetailed into the cotton system with ease. In some areas tenants were ignorant of the fact that there was a Bankhead Bill. Many of them had signed something but in the previous two years they had signed many sheets without knowing their meanings. In other areas they knowingly signed a trustees' agreement. The method employed by one planter indicates the practices sometimes resorted to:

> Mr. —— called all of us to the gin. He said, "We got to sign up with the government to gin our cotton this year. They're making us get tags for every bale and we can't gin none without them tags. I had a letter from the government to read to you but I left it at home. The government has appointed me trustee of your bale tags and all you have to do is bring the cotton to the gin as you always have. So everybody come and sign this paper so we can gin our cotton."

The tenants filed past and signed a trustees' agreement giving the planter the privilege he claimed had been given him by the government.

The net result of the program was that the landlords participated in the federal relief program and received the benefits it offered while the tenant merely obeyed the landlord's instructions. Federal relief came to the cotton belt, was translated into plantation terms and the system (except for the further displacement and impoverishment of tenants) was bolstered and given a new lease on life.

Tenants and Relief

It is not to be expected of a business with decreased production to use as much labor as it did when production was at a maximum. Five methods are in evidence for meeting the reduced need for tenant labor:

1. The tenant remains on the plantation eking out an existence from farming operations that are of such size as to be unprofitable.

2. The tenant remains on the plantation with his status changed to that of a casual laborer who has the privilege of producing what he can for family consumption.

3. The tenant occupies a house on the plantation but is supported by relief.

4. Unsatisfactory returns from his labors or artificially stimulated difficulties with the landlord force the tenant to move of his own volition to the small town.

5. Eviction from the farm by landlords who have no further need of his services.

Every available study of the position of the share tenants and croppers under the depression and the operation of the AAA corroborates in detail the observations here set down. Hoffsommer, in his study "The AAA and the Cropper," interviewed 800 landlords in 1934 and concluded that the economic relationship and the resulting social attitudes had made a situation in which it was difficult, if not impossible, for the government to deal directly with the cropper. The paternalism of the planter, the dependency of the tenant so meticulously maintained, the stern objections, on the part of the landlord, to any change in the traditional relationship, set up well nigh insurmountable barriers to any tenant benefits through this channel. In fact, 90 per cent of the landlords voiced opposition to any change, despite the impoverishment of these classes. Says Hoffsommer:

It appears... that this attitude arises from sentiment and tradition rather than from critical thought and planning on the basis of modern conditions. At any rate, the cropper is looked upon as a dependent person, the more extreme but not uncommon views regarding him as a class apart, incapable of ever achieving but a modicum of self-direction. Judged from his past achievements in climbing the so-called agricultural ladder, it would seem that superficially, at least, there is some justification for this view. In the Alabama study of those who started farming as share croppers, nearly three-fourths still remain such. Less than one-tenth have become owners.

There is a considerable feeling among landlords that anything which disturbs this dependent status of the cropper is undesirable. Forty per cent of the landlords in the above mentioned study stated, for example, that they were opposed to the granting of relief to these people because of its demoralizing effect upon them....

The share tenant's situation is the impossible one of being forced by the inadequacies of the present system, on the one hand, to seek relief as the only means of keeping alive; and, on the other hand, of having this relief opposed by the landlord because it may spoil him as a tenant, if and when he can be used again. There are other fears back of the landlord's attitude: the fear that the tenant will be removed from the influence of the landowner and learn that he is not entirely dependent on him; and the fear that the relief will raise the standard of living to the extent that bargaining on the old basis will be difficult. It can readily be seen that from the point of view of the landlord government relief is demoralizing.

Whatever the intention of the Government, it is apparent that the so-called parity payment turned out to be a mere farce and gesture to the share tenant and cropper. Under the 1934 revision of the landlord-tenant contract the share cropper receives one-half of the parity payments. But this is actually a very small sum. The share-cropper on a typical cotton farm of 12 acres, with 40 per cent of his acreage out of production, and assuming a base lint yield of 175 pounds per acre, would receive about $4.20 as his share, if he got that. Of 2,000 tenants studied in Alabama, 28 per cent of them received cotton benefit payments in 1933, and of the croppers and renters, 40 per cent paid over part of the money immediately to the landlord, and in a third of these cases this payment was actually forced by the landlords. It was found easier to force the Negroes to turn over their payments than the white tenants. Whereas force was used with 22 per cent of the whites, it was used with 58 per cent of the Negroes.

Dr. Calvin B. Hoover of the Department of Agriculture, in the course of his inquiries into the operation of the federal program, found the same condition. In summarizing his report he said:

Often these sums were legally due the landlord. In other cases, however, the interest rate which was charged was usurious and at a rate higher than that allowed by the laws of the State in which the parties to the contract lived. Whether the tenant received anything at all often depended upon the charitableness of the landlord. In numberless instances, if the landlord had deducted the entire sum which he had a legal right to do, there would have been no net amount received by the tenants at all. What apparently happened was that the deductions amounted sometimes to less than the legal amount due, sometimes to the amount legally due, depending upon the charitableness or unscrupulousness of the landlord.

In spite of the hopes expressed by the AAA that the landlord should keep so far as possible his accustomed number of tenants, this was not done; if it had been insisted upon the whole program was in danger of losing the support of the landlords. With the accelerated displacement of tenants, a movement that had already begun in 1929—reaching serious proportions in 1932—went also all prospects of "furnish" and shelter. The result is a homeless, shifting, and stranded population with no prospect of relief except that which might come from the government. In three counties in North Carolina, in an investigation made during the first four months of 1934, Gordon Blackwell of the University of North Carolina found 825 displaced tenant families. According to Mr. Blackwell:

... it appears that the problem first became serious in 1929 and 1930, the number of tenants displaced each year increasing until the peak year 1932. The number of families losing tenant status in 1933 was much lower than the figures for 1931 and 1932. In 1934, however, the upward trend is seen again, doubtless due to the acreage reduction program of the AAA...colored tenants were displaced slightly earlier than white tenants. A larger proportion of whites than Negroes has been displaced in 1934.

On the basis of his study, Mr. Blackwell estimated that in 1934 there were in North Carolina between 8,000 and 12,000 families who had been displaced and had no crops.

BENEFITS FOR OWNERS AND RELIEF FOR TENANTS

Most disturbing in the present relief efforts is the fact that in many areas the relief budgets for stranded families increase at the same time that benefit payments increase. Bolivar County, Mississippi, up to August 1, 1934, had received $380,394, the largest benefit payments in the state, yet from May 1933 to May 1934 the amount spent on relief in the county increased from $1,338 to $48,311. Sunflower County with benefit payments of $275,875, up to August 1, 1934, increased its relief expenditures from May 1933 to May 1934 from $5,668 to $32,325. For the same periods, Falls County, Texas, received $213,140 in benefits and in the year increased its relief expenditures from $2,992 to $8,892 per month. Its experience was duplicated by Dunklin County in the same state where $164,524 payment to

landowners was accompanied by a rise in relief costs
from $2,584 in May 1933 to $10,909 in May 1934.

Unless it is anticipated that federal relief is to be
permanent, some drastic measures are necessary now to
re-establish these stranded farmers' families on a sound
agricultural basis.

V

WHAT IS THE WAY OUT?

COMPOUNDED of bad economics and degrading social conditions, cotton culture faces sweeping changes. What is to become of the half-million to million families —the two million to five million individuals—who no longer are needed as cotton tenants? The alternatives seem to be (1) starvation, (2) permanent support on the relief rolls, (3) the finding of new work in the cities, (4) reorganization of farming in the old cotton states. The fourth is the only acceptable and feasible choice. We cannot allow hundreds of thousands of our fellow citizens to starve; permanent support on the relief rolls of millions of able-bodied farmers is out of the question; the cities and their industries are already overcrowded and probably cannot in the future absorb the normal increases of farm population, let alone a sudden inrush of millions of dispossessed farm laborers. Some reorganization of farming in the cotton states must be devised whereby these former tenants can make their own livelihood and develop a self-respecting as well as self-supporting way of life.

The pressing needs of the millions of tenants, whose

lives have always been barren and precarious, and who now find themselves dispossessed from even the poor living they formerly had, can be met only by some new distribution of land ownership. Here in briefest outline are the suggestions which have been advanced almost unanimously by students of farm problems, southern statesmen, and government officials.

1. That the federal government (through some special agency set up for that purpose) buy up huge acreages of farm lands now in the hands of insurance companies, land banks, and others, and distribute this land in small plots of minimum size required to support farm families, probably twenty to forty acres in the cotton area. The land may be allocated to the new owners either on long leases or through contracts of sale on long-time payment under easy terms. The aim is to give the new farmers a sense of ownership or stability and to prevent them from selling or mortgaging the holdings or otherwise alienating their new birthright.

2. That service agencies be set up by regions and local areas to supervise, guide, and aid the new homesteaders. These service agencies should not only give expert counsel but also provide seed, fertilizer, and even certain of the current supplies which were heretofore furnished by the plantation owner. In certain instances the service agencies will have to finance buildings and farm animals, but these capital investments should be held to the very minimum so that the

homesteaders will not start with too burdensome a
debt. It is believed that the project can succeed on a
large scale only if the capital investment (including
land and whatever buildings, repairs, and animals are
required) does not exceed one thousand dollars to
fifteen hundred dollars per family.

3. That along with this general wide-scale distribution of lands, experiments be conducted in unified
and carefully directed types of communities, such as
(a) coöperative farm colonies, (b) communities with
highly developed services in schools and health and
recreational facilities, also with community incubators,
breeding stock, and marketing facilities, and (c) communities of the European type with homes and public
services concentrated into villages with farm lands on
the outskirts.

The Re-homesteading Project is intended to establish
in farm ownership a huge number of families heretofore
excluded from ownership and now being cut off even
from tenancy or crop-sharing arrangements. To this end
the provisions and stipulations must be few and simple.

Success will depend largely on the low cost of the
capital investment to each homesteader and on the re-
sourcefulness, helpfulness, and honesty of the service
agencies in supplying central services, carrying the families until the first crops are in, and guiding the homesteaders both as individuals and as communities. Schools,
health facilities, and other public services will continue

to be furnished by the state, county, and district authorities as at present, but the new service agencies probably can do much to improve or make more effective these services in the new communities of homesteaders.

The benefits are almost self-evident. First, hundreds of thousands of families will have a little land of their own. The effect of land-ownership is striking and immediate in creating self-respect and stability. Second, the chief interest of a small farm owner is to raise food and supplies for his own use. A well-rounded diet and resulting improvements in health will come quickly if farm families are raising meat and vegetables and producing milk and eggs for their own tables.

These small farm owners will not be stopped from growing their quota of cotton or of any other commercial crop, since they must have some income to buy clothes and shoes, and shelter and food beyond what they themselves can produce. But the chief efforts of these new homesteaders will be toward growing foodstuffs for their own consumption and making things for their own use. Furthermore, many new cash crops can be developed: grapes, fruits, truck and dairy produce for nearby cities, livestock, and other new crops. A great variety of salable farm produce, needed in the South and throughout the country, can supplement cotton as a means of income.

Fortunately, these proposals are not entirely in the state of mere pious hopes. Through the federal and state relief administrations farm distribution, in general accord with the plans outlined above, has already proceeded to some extent in several of the cotton states. Through the large appropriation for public works voted by Congress in the spring of 1935, additional sums are made available for rural rehabilitation and resettlement. This will make possible expansion of the project for small farm ownership, and provide through work relief for the building and repair of homes and barns, of schools and other community centers. Congress has before it a bill authorizing an issue of bonds to finance individual farm purchases on a wide scale. It looks very much as though, by these and other means, broad and effective measures may be taken to mitigate the tenancy evil and to rehabilitate great numbers of the population as self-supporting and self-respecting farmers.

It is of course not to be supposed that this scheme of land distribution, even if carried out wisely and on a wide scale, will solve all the problems of the rural South. There remain such severe ills as (1) large stretches of worn-out soil, (2) the long tradition of concentration on the single cash crop, cotton, which the new farmers will find it hard to break away from, (3) the vicious and enervating prejudice between the races which beclouds issues and makes almost impossible any concerted program of recovery and progress, and (4) the traditions of dependence and the general shiftlessness and incompetence of the workers, both white and

colored, who make up the large marginal farm population. But organization of the farm system is basic to
reform in other matters. A group of independent farmers working together under competent leadership can
begin to plan decent lives as well as a self-sustaining
economy.

Most civilized nations of the world long ago faced
the problem of tenancy and developed far-reaching
measures to reorganize this backward system of land
tenure. Denmark systematically abolished tenancy completely, Ireland and Germany and Mexico have made
drastic reforms. In the United States nothing of a serious and far-reaching character has been done to modify
an admittedly wretched agrarian system. Secretary Wal-
lace has expressed himself unqualifiedly on the dangers
of tenancy when he says:

> It seems to me that it will be virtually impossible
> for America to develop a rural civilization which
> affords security, opportunity, and a fully abundant life
> for our rural people unless she acts to convert tenants
> of this sort into owner farmers.

APPENDIX

LEGAL STATUS OF THE SHARE TENANT

THE wide variation in practice and the acute difficulties in landlord-tenant relations throughout the South force some consideration of the legal status of share tenants. The legal relationship of employer-employee exists when the employer possesses the right to select and discharge the employee and to direct what work shall be done and the way it shall be done. Since the tenant or cropper furnishes no part of the capital, he has no claim in law upon the product beyond the established laborer's lien. Throughout the South, however, the landlord lien laws enacted have provided that the landowner possesses a prior lien, whether contracted or not on the tenant's crop covering rent, and all advances of cash, supplies, feed, and equipment. Designed to protect the landlord against dishonest tenants seeking to evade payment of debts, both the law and custom limit the rights of all tenants even in respect to the laborer's lien. One important North Carolina decision (State *vs.* Austin) refers to a share tenant as "a servant whose wages depend upon the amount of profit." In Georgia and South Carolina all share tenants are legally classed as croppers and have no title to "the crops they grow."

This is merely a crystallization into law of customary practices on the assumption that in dealing with share tenants only Negroes are involved. But the fact is that in Georgia 65,104 Negro croppers and other share tenants fall under this classification, and 81,753 white croppers and share tenants!

Texas, representing the newer cotton areas, escaped some of the tradition of southeastern plantation states, and is characterized by larger proportions of white tenancy. This variance from the familiar pattern of the Old South was registered

71

promptly in conflicts between landlords and tenants unheard of in the Old South. Tenant contracts actually reached the point of political discussion and some protective legislation. Where custom could not be relied upon to determine the tenant's status beyond the one-fourth cotton share rent, landlords had begun to demand bonus rents in excess of the expected share. Such violent reactions followed the practice that in 1910 a Renters Union was organized precipitating a situation which resulted in an investigation of the land problem by the Industrial Relations Commissioner of the United States Senate. A law limiting rentals followed, making illegal the collection of over half of all the crops where the landlord furnished only the land. But even in this state where some protective legislation has been enacted, only the renter is affected and this class is not merely the least numerous but is nearest ownership status. Of 301,660 tenants in Texas only 16,874 are cash tenants, or renters.

In the southeastern cotton states the condition remains as it has always been, and the status of the tenant has in 1935 been reaffirmed in a recent Arkansas decision. In a suit brought by share croppers to recover a laborer's lien in the benefit payments under the AAA, the share-cropper is declared to be only a third party to the contract, that is, that he is merely a factor about which the two principals have made an agreement.

TABLE I

CLASSES OF FARM OPERATORS IN TEN PRINCIPAL COTTON GROWING STATES IN 1930 WHITE AND COLORED COMBINED

	Full Owners	Part Owners	Managers	Tenants Cash	Tenants Others	All Kinds
North Carolina	115,765	25,680	648	9,237	128,378	279,708
South Carolina	45,515	8,955	693	18,270	84,498	157,931
Georgia	70,596	9,206	1,406	27,533	146,857	255,598
Tennessee	109,853	21,673	611	12,216	101,304	245,657
Alabama	75,144	15,228	603	48,707	117,713	257,395
Mississippi	77,382	8,665	999	27,103	198,514	312,663
Arkansas	72,597	16,412	634	14,961	137,730	242,334
Louisiana	46,893	6,266	735	12,886	94,665	161,445
Oklahoma	53,647	24,067	823	17,598	107,731	203,866
Texas	152,852	37,663	3,314	16,874	284,786	495,489
TOTAL TEN STATES	820,244	173,815	10,466	205,385	1,402,176	2,612,086

73

Types of Tenancy *

Share Cropping for Half and Half	Share Renting for Third and Fourth	Cash or Standing Renting

Landlord Furnishes:

Land	Land	Land
House	House	House
Fuel	Fuel	Fuel
Tools	One fourth or one third of Fertilizers	
Work Stock		
Feed for Stock		
Seed		
One half of Fertilizer		

Tenant Furnishes:

Labor	Labor	Labor
One half of Fertilizer	Work Stock	Work Stock
	Food for Stock	Food for Stock
	Tools	Tools
	Seed	Seed
	Three fourths or two thirds of Fertilizer	Fertilizers

Landlord Gets:

One half of crop	One fourth or one third of crop	Fixed amount in cash or cotton

Tenant Gets:

One half of crop	Three fourths or two thirds of crop	Entire crop less fixed amount

* E. A. Goldenweiser and E. A. Boeger: *A Study of the Tenant Systems of Farming in the Yazoo-Mississippi Delta*, U. S. Department of Agriculture, Bulletin 337.

TABLE II

EARNINGS OF SHARE CROPPERS AND SHARE TENANTS IN 1933, IN SIX SELECTED COUNTIES *

Share Croppers

Area	Average No. Bales Produced	Average Gross Earnings	Rent	Operator's Gross
Bolivar (Miss.)	9.4	$451.20	$225.60	$225.60
Noxubee (Miss.)	3.2	153.60	76.80	76.80
Harrison (Texas) ...	3.7	166.50	83.75	83.75
Fort Bend (Texas) ..	10.6	477.00	238.50	238.50
Laurens (S. C.)	10.4	488.50	244.40	244.40
Marlboro (S. C.)	17.5	822.50	584.32	238.18

Share Tenants

Area	Average No. Bales Produced	Average Gross Earnings	Rent	Operator's Gross
Bolivar (Miss.)	13.6	$652.80	$163.20	$489.60
Noxubee (Miss.)	4.0	192.00	48.00	144.00
Harrison (Texas) ...	3.7	166.50	41.63	124.87
Fort Bend (Texas) ..	7.9	355.50	88.87	266.63
Laurens (S. C.)	(Too few cases for sample)			
Marlboro (S. C.)	13.5	634.50	317.25	317.25

* From study of 2,000 tenant families by the Committee on Minority Groups in the Economic Recovery.

TABLE III

ECONOMIC STATUS AND RESULTANT SOCIAL STATUS OF DIFFERENT ECONOMIC CLASSES IN TYPICAL TENANT CROPPER AREA*

	Operator Landlords		Owner Operators		Tenants		Croppers	
	White	Black	White	Black	White	Black	White	Black
Equity per family	$14,494	$8,974	$3,998	$3,908	$886	$226	$352	$126
Equity per person......	2,750	1,019	889.00	597.00	177.40	37.68	72.15	24.83
Per cent who are insolvent	0	0	0	0	6.5	28.5	24.2	18.75
Annual Cash income per individual	425.65	226.82	253.82	253.03	174.45	118.51	143.13	125.64
Average number of rooms per home	5.6	3.8	4.5	3.8	4.2	4.0	4.1	3.4
Per cent of homes with running water	6.6	0	0	0	0	0	1.7	0
Per cent of homes with lights other than oil lamps	10.2	0	0	0	3.5	0	1.7	0

*Rupert B. Vance, *Human Geography of the South*, The University of North Carolina Press, 1932, p. 202. (Data from Economic and Social Conditions of North Carolina Farmers, Carl C. Taylor and C. C. Zimmerman, Bureau of Economics and Social Research, North Carolina State College of Agriculture, Raleigh, North Carolina, 1922.)

76

Per cent of homes with kitchen sinks	10.2	20.0	0	0	1.3	0	0	0
Per cent of births at which doctor was in attendance	76.0	33.3	72.5	28.6	57.5	8.3	48.0	14.6
Per cent of parents who can read and write	81.8	80.0	80.0	90.0	86.5	35.8	70.8	42.3
Per cent of families who take papers and magazines	83.4	60.0	65.0	60.0	55.4	7.4	50.0	17.9
Average number of books in homes	15.2	0.8	1.4	20.2	2.69	1.5	2.24	0.6
Number of times members of family have participated in recreation during year	3.04	.79	1.73	1.97	1.40	.25	.92	.88
Per cent of families who own automobiles	92.9	60.0	45.0	60.0	49.4	14.3	34.5	16.96
Per cent of parents in favor of consolidated schools, road bonds, college education, etc.	59.4	36.7	46.7	73.5	45.3	14.3	14.1	17.4

SELECTED BIBLIOGRAPHY

THE following books, journals, and reports are recommended to any persons who may wish to acquaint themselves somewhat fully with one or another aspect of cotton culture in the United States. Far from exhaustive, this list is given simply as a guide to easily accessible and authoritative material for the general reader.

BOOKS

Baker, Ray Stannard. *Following the Color Line*, New York, Doubleday, Page & Company, 1908.

Barbee, William J. *The Cotton Question*, New York, Metropolitan Record Office, 1866.

Bizzell, William Bennett. *Farm Tenantry*, Texas Agricultural Experiment Station, 1921.

Black, John Donald. *Agricultural Reform in the United States*, New York, McGraw-Hill Publishing Company, 1929.

Brooks, Robert P. *The Agrarian Revolution in Georgia*, Madison, Wis., 1914.

Couch, W. T. (Ed.). *Culture in the South*, Chapel Hill, The University of North Carolina Press, 1934.

Dodd, William Edward. *The Cotton Kingdom*, New Haven, Yale University Press, 1921.

Elliot, Clara D. *The Farmers' Campaign for Credit*, New York, D. Appleton Co., 1927.

Galpin, Charles J. *Rural Social Problems*, New York, The Century Company, 1924.

Gillette, John M. *Rural Sociology*, New York, The Macmillan Company, 1928.

Hawthorne, Horace B. *The Sociology of Rural Life*, New York, The Century Company, 1926.

Heer, Clarence. *Income and Wages in the South*, Chapel Hill, The University of North Carolina Press, 1930.

Herrick, Myron Timothy. *Rural Credits*, New York, D. Appleton and Co., 1928.

Hoffer, Charles R. *Introduction to Rural Sociology*, New York, Richard R. Smith, 1930.

Hubbard, William Hustace. *Cotton and the Cotton Market*, New York, D. Appleton & Company, 1927.

Johnson, Charles S. *Shadow of the Plantation*, Chicago, The University of Chicago Press, 1934.

Lee, Virgil Porter. *Principles of Agricultural Credit*, New York, McGraw-Hill Publishing Company, 1930.

Phillips, Chester Arthur. *Bank Credit*, New York, Macmillan Company, 1920.

Tannenbaum, Frank. *Darker Phases of the South*, New York, G. P. Putnam, 1924.

Taylor, H. C. *Outlines of Agricultural Economics*, New York, Macmillan Company, 1931.

Warren, George Frederick, and Pearson, F. A. *Prices*, New York, John Wiley, 1933.

Vance, Rupert. *Human Geography in the South*, Chapel Hill, The University of North Carolina Press, 1932.

———. *Human Factors in Cotton Culture*, Chapel Hill, The University of North Carolina Press, 1929.

———. *Regional Reconstruction: A Way Out for the South*, Chapel Hill, Foreign Policy Association and the University of North Carolina Press, 1935.

Yarborough, William A. *Economic Aspects of Slavery in Relation to Southern and Southwestern Migration*, Nashville, Tennessee. George Peabody College for Teachers, 1932.

"The American Negro," *Annals of the American Academy of Political and Social Science*, vol. CXXXX (November, 1928).

ARTICLES IN JOURNALS

Blackwell, Gordon W. "The Displaced Tenant Farm Family in North Carolina," *Journal of Social Forces*, XIII (October, 1934), 65-73.

Branson, E. C. "Farm Tenancy in the Cotton Belt: How Farm Tenants Live," *Journal of Social Forces*, I (March, 1923), 213-21.

Eustler, Roland B. "Agricultural Credit and the Negro Farmer," *Journal of Social Forces*, VIII (March, 1930), 416-25; VIII (June, 1930), 565-73.

Hoffsommer, Harold. "The AAA and the Cropper," *Journal of Social Forces*, XIII (May, 1935), 494-502.

Kemmerer, Edwin Walter. "Agricultural Credit in the United States," *American Economic Review*, II (December, 1912), 852-72.

Snyder, H. "Negro Migration and the Cotton Crop," *North American Review*, CCXIX (January, 1924), 21-29.

Stephens, P. H. "Mechanization of Cotton Farms," *Journal of Farm Economics*, XIII (January, 1931), 27-36.

REPORTS

Annals of the American Academy of Political and Social Science: "The Agricultural Situation in the United States," January, 1925.

Annual Reports of the Comptroller of the Currency.

Annual Reports of the Federal Farm Loan Board.

Annual Reports of the Federal Reserve Board.

Business Men's Commission of Agriculture: *The Condition of Agriculture in the United States and Measures for its Improvement.* A report of the Chamber of Commerce of the United States. National Industrial Conference Board. 1927.

Gray, L. C. "Credit Problems of the Southern Plantation System." International Conference on Marketing and Farm Credits. 1916.

Olsen, Nils H., and Brannen, G. F. "Farm Credit." *United States Department of Agriculture Yearbooks.* 1921; 1924.